ROSE LEWENSTEIN

Theatre includes *Darknet* (Southwark Playh... (Women@RADA); *Now This Is Not The End* (Arcoₗ... *Life* (The Yard); *Only Human* (Theatre503) and *Ain't No Law Against Fish 'n' Chips* (Royal Court Young Writers' Festival). Television includes *That Girl* as part of drama anthology *On the Edge* (BlackLight/Channel 4). Rose is currently under commission to the Royal Court Theatre and is developing original TV dramas with Kudos, Hillbilly, Red, Snowed-In, Euston Films and Wild Mercury, as well as adaptations of *The Gender Games* (SunnyMarch) and *Flatshare* (42).

Rose Lewenstein

COUGAR

NICK HERN BOOKS
London
www.nickhernbooks.co.uk

A Nick Hern Book

Cougar first published in Great Britain as a paperback original in 2019 by Nick Hern Books Limited, The Glasshouse, 49a Goldhawk Road, London W12 8QP, in association with the Orange Tree Theatre, Richmond

Cougar copyright © 2019 Rose Lewenstein

Rose Lewenstein has asserted her right to be identified as the author of this work

Cover image: www.istockphoto.com/ptaxa

Designed and typeset by Nick Hern Books, London
Printed in the UK by Mimeo Ltd, Huntingdon, Cambridgeshire PE29 6XX

A CIP catalogue record for this book is available from the British Library

ISBN 978 1 84842 812 6

Woodland
CARBON
www.woodlandcarbon.co.uk
NICK HERN BOOKS
Printed on Carbon Captured paper

Cougar was first performed at the Orange Tree Theatre, Richmond, on 1 February 2019. The cast was as follows:

JOHN	Mike Noble
LEILA	Charlotte Randle

Director	Chelsea Walker
Designer	Rosanna Vize
Lighting Designer	Jess Bernberg
Sound Designer	Alexandra Faye Braithwaite
& Composer	
Movement Director	Shelley Maxwell
Casting Consultant	Annelie Powell CDG

Acknowledgements

Thanks to Richard Twyman for asking me to write a play and
reading early drafts; Chelsea Walker for finding it, developing it
and making it happen; Paul Miller for believing in it and taking a
risk; everyone at the Orange Tree and English Touring Theatre
for all their support; Harriet Pennington Legh for reading every
draft of everything; Guy Jones for dramaturgy; Leonie Mellinger
for thoughts and insights; Chris Campbell for emotional journeys;
and Charlotte Randle, Mike Noble and the creative team for
bringing the play to life.

R.L.

Characters

LEILA, *mid-forties*
JOHN, *mid-twenties*
BUTLER/YOUNG MAN, *early twenties*

Notes

(*) *indicates a jump in time and place*

This text went to press before the end of rehearsals and so may differ slightly from the play as performed.

A hotel room – expensive and soulless.

JOHN *is asleep in bed.* LEILA *watches him sleep.*

*

He wakes.

LEILA   Morning.

JOHN   Is it?

LEILA   Sleep well?

JOHN   Actually I

LEILA   Had to move you onto your side.

JOHN

LEILA   You were snoring.

JOHN   Oh.

LEILA   A lot.

JOHN   Sorry.

Sorry about that, I think there's something

wrong, with my sinus, it's a medical condition – swollen turbinate? There's this procedure I could have but

LEILA   You were drinking.

JOHN   Hm?

LEILA   A lot.

JOHN   Huh.

Sorry can I just

She takes off her bathrobe. Starts getting dressed.

He watches her. She can feel him watching her.

Sorry

can I just

check

LEILA

JOHN   Did we

LEILA   No.

JOHN   Right.

Just checking.

So um

Were we ever going to

LEILA   No.

JOHN   Yeah. No. Good.

So I didn't fuck up my chances by

LEILA   falling asleep?

JOHN   Yeah.

LEILA   No.

JOHN   Good.

LEILA

JOHN   No, I just mean if we had, you know

LEILA

JOHN   Well I'd want to know about it, I'd want it
         saved. In my memory.

*

LEILA   I know some people enjoy it, the anticipation, but
          really I've got enough to worry about with this speech

JOHN   Course.

LEILA   and I like to get it over with.

JOHN

LEILA   The sex.

JOHN   Oh.

          Okay.

LEILA   Okay?

JOHN   I didn't assume

LEILA   Didn't you?

JOHN   I'm not really

          allowed to assume, that sort of thing, it's little bit

          problematic, to assume those sorts of things.

LEILA   Is it?

JOHN   I mean

LEILA   even if you don't act on it?

JOHN   What?

LEILA   even if it's only in your head?

*

He slaps himself across the face.

LEILA   What are you doing?

JOHN   Just checking

          that I'm not, you know

          asleep.

LEILA   You're not.

JOHN   I have these dreams, sometimes I can't tell if I'm

LEILA   You're awake.

JOHN   Yeah but sometimes, in the dreams, sometimes the characters they try and trick me, they say things like

LEILA   Trust me.

JOHN

LEILA   Look in the mirror.

JOHN

LEILA   Reflections are blurry in dreams.

        He looks in the mirror.

JOHN   Huh.

        Yeah, no, you're right, I am definitely

        awake, I had some

        Clothes. They're in a pile on the floor.

        He gets dressed – quickly, awkwardly.

        Sorry

        can I just

        Who are you and

        why? am I here?

*

LEILA   Leila.

JOHN   John.

*

JOHN   There was this one time, few years ago, I got a night bus home from work and the next thing I knew it was six in the morning and I was in a bus depot in Edmonton and the driver was shaking me awake and my hair was all wet from the condensation on the window and

        You have Great hair.

LEILA I know.

JOHN Have you ever been to Edmonton?

LEILA No.

JOHN No, didn't think so.

It was just a few hours but it felt like I'd lost days. Weeks.

This though, waking up here

This is nothing like Edmonton.

Why was I

Oh yeah, the night bus, I'm not an alcoholic by the way – God you're really fucking beautiful, have you tried the eggs Benedict?

LEILA I'm a vegetarian.

JOHN Oh.

That's a shame because it really is exceptional, I believe it was voted best eggs Benedict in the country? maybe even the world and look if it makes a difference I think the pig led a very happy life

LEILA Oh I don't care about the pig.

JOHN Oh.

Okay.

Well listen, don't bother calling room service, he knows me, the chef, I can just go down to the kitchen and

LEILA

JOHN Did he say the word fired? Did he actually say fired?

*

JOHN If I'd known, when I had the ice bucket, when I was this close

LEILA

JOHN   Said you liked it. The violence.

LEILA   I did. I do. But.

        I'm not an egg.

        a china doll.

        If you smash me I won't break.

        D'you understand?

*

JOHN   I caught bits of it.

LEILA

JOHN   The conference.

        But I couldn't tell you what it was about.

LEILA   Mitigation and Adaptation.

JOHN   You know when words are just words

LEILA   They're two different approaches

JOHN   to banking?

LEILA   to climate change.

JOHN   Could've sworn they were bankers.

LEILA   It's an auditing firm, they're financial auditors.

JOHN   Financial auditors, saving the planet one conference at a time.

LEILA   It's called corporate sustainability.

JOHN   Sounds like an oxymoron.

LEILA   It's my job. It's what I do.

*

JOHN   Well it was nice to meet you

LEILA   Leila.

JOHN   John.

And thanks. For letting me stay in your bed. I never
get to see the rooms.

LEILA   No?

JOHN   No, there's like a total divide between bar staff and
housekeeping, we don't even talk to each other, I mean
most of them can't speak English, I mean that's not
Why we don't talk, I'm not

I want you to know

What I did last night, that's not

typical behaviour of mine, that's not a Me kind of
thing to do.

You guys wasted a lot of wine. Red, white

And I don't like waste. Can't stand waste.

So I drank it.

And I don't know what came over me but I think maybe
that's what people mean when they say See Red.

Right, well, I better

LEILA   Be careful.

JOHN   Bit of rain never

LEILA   There's a red-level warning.

JOHN   London's drowning, is it?

LEILA   Couldn't get a taxi last night.

JOHN   Think I'll just jump on a

LEILA   That's why I stayed, after the conference.

That's why You stayed, after you hit my colleague over
the head with an ice bucket and called him a cunt.

JOHN   That was

         your colleague

         Right.

LEILA   I mean he is a cunt.

JOHN   Right.

LEILA   But he didn't press charges, so

*

JOHN   What did he do to you?

LEILA   You really want to know?

JOHN

LEILA   It happened. I was there. He Did To Me – I don't

         That's not how I choose to think about it.

*

LEILA   I thought about touching you while you were passed out.

JOHN

LEILA   I didn't.

JOHN

LEILA   What do you think about that?

JOHN   I think

         that's weird. Why are you telling me that? that's weird.

LEILA   Is it?

JOHN   Yes.

         If I said that to you

LEILA

JOHN

LEILA

JOHN   Right, well, I better

find a job or

stop drinking or

LEILA   Come with me.

JOHN   What?

LEILA   Conference next week.

JOHN   Where?

LEILA   Rio, I'm giving a speech.

JOHN   I've just been fired, I can't afford

LEILA   Air miles.

JOHN

LEILA   No, of course, it's

silly, I didn't mean to make you feel

JOHN   No

LEILA   uncomfortable.

JOHN   you didn't, I'm not, and I'm fine with women paying
for stuff, and I've never been to Rio, it's more just

I don't know you, I mean who are you? I mean

LEILA

JOHN   Are you married?

*

JOHN   I have a right to know.

LEILA   Do you?

JOHN   I have

I think when you invest this much

Self, you have rights, you have

LEILA   No. My story. My choice. I get to choose.

*

Series of checks. She sits on the bed. Too hard. Paces across the room. Too small. Checks the view from the window. Wrong aspect.

Picks up the guest phone. Dials and waits.

JOHN   This is fine, this is more than fine

LEILA   (*Into phone.*) Yes I'd like to speak to the manager.

*

JOHN   I thought the other room was fine

LEILA   I don't want fine.

JOHN   I thought it was more than fine

LEILA   I don't pay for fine.

JOHN   You don't pay for any of it, do you?

LEILA   It was facing the wrong way for a start – they can bring that up for you, you don't have to

JOHN   I can carry my own bag, it's

fine – fuck me, that sunset, feels like we're on a different planet.

He drops his bag. Takes it in.

I downloaded the Lonely Planet app.

I wanna see some stuff, you know?

LEILA   Stuff?

JOHN   Real stuff. Like I wanna dance to real samba and eat those deep-fried cheese-ball things and go inside a favela in Santa Marta and buy drugs off a boy with no shoes on.

(*Reading from his phone.*) It says that today, the neighbourhood is a mixture of chaos and beauty. After dark, prostitutes trawl the restaurants along Atlantica while overstimulated foreigners stumble towards the strip clubs around Princesa Isabel

LEILA   Well, knock yourself out.

JOHN   I wouldn't describe myself as an overstimulated foreigner, that's not how I'd describe myself.

LEILA   How would you describe yourself?

JOHN   Um

        Okay, three words

        Adventurous. Loyal.

        Sound like a dog, don't I? can't think of a third.

LEILA   And how would you describe me?

JOHN   Okay, first impressions, three words

        Completely fucking impenetrable.

*

LEILA   I know I'm not supposed to like it but I did. I found it attractive. The violence. The spirit of it.

*

LEILA   Are you consenting to this?

JOHN   This?

LEILA   Sex. With me.

JOHN   I mean

LEILA   This isn't a transaction

JOHN   I want to, obviously

LEILA   but I like things to be clear.

JOHN   I mean as well as the sightseeing

LEILA   Why obviously?

JOHN   Well, because you're

LEILA

JOHN   and I'm

LEILA

JOHN   You were saying?

LEILA   I like to get it over with.

JOHN   Okay.

LEILA   Okay?

JOHN   Right now?

LEILA   Would you like a drink first?

JOHN   What?

LEILA   Would you like

JOHN   a drink

LEILA   Yes.

JOHN   Yes.

LEILA   Help yourself.

JOHN

LEILA   The minibar.

JOHN   Right.

> *He opens the minibar. Pours himself a Scotch.*
>
> Want one?

LEILA   I shouldn't.

JOHN

LEILA   The speech.

JOHN   Course.

LEILA   There's ice in the

JOHN   Thanks.

*

LEILA   I get nervous, my throat tightens up, my palms go all
         sweaty

JOHN   You'll be fine.

LEILA   I know I'll be fine, I'm always fine, doesn't mean I don't hate it.

JOHN   So why d'you do it?

LEILA   I'm the fucking expert.

JOHN   But if you hate public speaking that much

LEILA   I don't know.

JOHN   why put yourself through that?

LEILA   Well, I suppose

I like to scare myself.

JOHN   Practise on me.

LEILA   What? No.

JOHN   Go on, I'll run lines with you.

LEILA   Lines aren't the problem.

JOHN   I'll be your audience.

*

LEILA   Right, well

JOHN   I better

LEILA   Probably for the best.

JOHN   Probably is.

He turns to leave.

Stops.

People are always saying carpe diem, seize the day, live each moment to the full, grab life by the bollocks, I'd like to come with you.

LEILA   Okay.

JOHN   I don't have any money.

LEILA   I know.

JOHN   Okay.

*

LEILA   Fine.

Our latest report shows that the required improvement in global carbon intensity has been limited to a one-point-five degree warming target to achieve net zero levels by

Is this boring, am I boring you?

JOHN   No, it's

LEILA   Fine.

We are contemplating a much more challenging future.

What will the world look like if we fail to rapidly decarbonise the global economy? and then I talk a bit about businesses engaging in materially relevant areas and the removal of industrial emissions and investment in lower-carbon nuclear power and sustainable initiatives in developing countries and

JOHN   What will it look like?

LEILA

JOHN   The world. If we fail to

LEILA   rapidly decarbonise the global economy?

JOHN   Yeah.

LEILA   Well, I suppose

Heat. Drought. Flooding. Environmental refugees. Extinction.

JOHN   That's

quite shit really.

LEILA   I'm building to the Green Agenda. That's why I'm here, that's why I'm speaking. Put simply, the Green Agenda gives you, the company, the chance to invest in sustainable activities while at the same time maximising profits

JOHN   So me, the company, will only invest in sustainable activities if it's profitable.

LEILA   Exactly.

JOHN   Huh.

LEILA   and then I end with the line, This is about thinking long term and acting short term.

JOHN   I don't know what that means.

LEILA   That's because you are not my audience.

She opens a mini-bottle of white wine. Drinks straight from the bottle.

It's not exactly what I thought I'd be doing. When I finished my PhD I was thinking charity, NGO, that sort of thing.

But where there's money there's influence there's change.

JOHN   If you can't beat 'em

LEILA   No. It isn't black and white. Bottom line is I'm doing a good thing.

*

JOHN   I didn't assume

LEILA   Didn't you?

JOHN   I'm not really

LEILA   Shh.

JOHN   allowed

LEILA   Stop talking.

JOHN   This is

       I mean

       Is this

       good?

LEILA   You're still talking.

JOHN   Sorry.

LEILA   You say sorry a lot.

JOHN   I apologise for that.

LEILA   (*Whispered.*) Shut up.

       A look – electric.

       Wait.

JOHN

LEILA   Just promise me you won't

       you know

JOHN

LEILA   fall in love.

*

Lightning strikes.

LEILA   When you touch me I get these shivers.

JOHN   When you shiver I

       something

       in my chest – fuck, that sounds

LEILA   I'm sure it's normal, just

       I can't remember it

       happening

       before

JOHN   These Midwestern storms, they're

LEILA   intense.

JOHN   If the world ends I want it to be here, with you.

LEILA   The world won't end. Not yet.

JOHN   I don't want this to end. This moment I mean, not

LEILA   It feels like this because it isn't real.

JOHN   Look in the mirror.

LEILA   It'll fade once we're back. The shivers. That feeling in
          your chest.

JOHN   Is that how it works?

LEILA   Until next time. That's how it has to work. That's
          the deal.

JOHN   Deal.

LEILA   You carry on with your life and I

JOHN   What life?

*

LEILA   I want to, obviously

JOHN   but you like things to be

LEILA   clear, yes, I mean

JOHN   Why obviously?

LEILA   Well, because you're

JOHN

LEILA   and I'm

*

She checks the time.

LEILA   Fuck.

          That can't be the time.

JOHN   Mm?

LEILA   That doesn't feel like the time.

JOHN   Mm.

She gets up. Starts getting dressed.

LEILA   I'm never late. It's not Me to be late.

JOHN   Maybe they'll start late.

LEILA   They're German, of course they won't start late.

JOHN   Maybe something terrible will happen and the roads will close and they'll have to postpone it.

LEILA   Go back to sleep.

JOHN   Or call in sick. I'll do it if you want – honestly, I'm really good at calling in sick.

LEILA   Really.

JOHN   Really, I'm honestly really good at making up tragic excuses that no one can argue with. My mum died about fifteen times last year.

She is actually dead so it's not like I'm tempting fate.

She'd find it funny. I think.

LEILA   Yes, hilarious as that sounds, and I'm sure you're very convincing

JOHN   I am.

LEILA   but you're talking about bartending

JOHN   and catering and call centres

LEILA   and I'm talking about legislation on greenhouse gas monitoring

JOHN   Sounds important.

LEILA   and so I don't think Calling In Sick is going to cut it.

*

JOHN   I went for a walk. Saw a handwritten poster pinned to a lamp post, it was advertising a house – some farm, somewhere remote, dirty pond and these awful yellow chairs and it looked like a scene from a horror film but I found myself wanting to call the number and for us to just

disappear.

together.

*

JOHN   You around for lunch?

LEILA   Possibly.

JOHN   I might visit the Museo de Arte Contemporáneo.

Or I might use the pool.

Looked nice, didn't it? the pool?

LEILA   Very nice.

JOHN   Yeah.

Yeah be good to know if you're around for lunch or not. Would help inform my decision R E the museo or the pool.

LEILA   I said possibly.

JOHN   Okay.

I might use the pool then.

LEILA   Okay.

JOHN   So yeah if I don't pick up it's because I'm 'using the pool'.

LEILA   Fine.

JOHN   Swimming in it.

LEILA   I gathered.

JOHN   I like swimming.

*

LEILA   I like watching you sleep.

JOHN   I don't like it that we waste time sleeping.

LEILA   I like feeling

normal.

JOHN   You're not normal. You're extraordinary. When you speak

you're like this VIP, this climate-change celebrity, it's

LEILA   silly.

JOHN   extraordinary.

LEILA   It's my job. It's what I do.

JOHN   I want to do things to you. I mean for you. I mean

I want to write you letters, I want to sing to you in French

*

She checks the time.

LEILA   Fuck.

That can't be the

JOHN   Look at the sky.

LEILA   I don't have time to look at the sky.

JOHN   Great big fuck-off cloud but there's a cartoon sun on the weather app.

LEILA   Weather is a chaotic system.

JOHN   It's like the meteorologists do it on purpose to mess with my head.

LEILA   Google nonlinear dynamics.

JOHN   Would you care if I disappeared?

LEILA   Have you seen my shoes?

JOHN   if I got hit by a car or drowned in the pool or just

LEILA   Nude ones with the pointy heels, I was wearing them
last night.

JOHN   evaporated into thin air?

LEILA   Was I?

JOHN   would you miss me?

LEILA   wearing them last night?

She crawls under the bed.

JOHN   You have so many shoes, I've never met anyone who
not only owns but travels with as many pairs of shoes
as you do. How many more pairs of shoes do you have
at home or do you take them all with you?

*She reappears with the shoes. Puts them on. Adjusts
her dress.*

LEILA   This look alright?

JOHN   Yup.

LEILA   Not too young?

JOHN   Nope.

LEILA   Not too old?

JOHN   I don't

think so, what is the correct

LEILA   I would.

Miss you

if you disappeared.

I want you here.

JOHN   Just here?

LEILA   I'm

in a hurry and we talked about this, John.

JOHN   No, I know

LEILA   I pay. Your flights, your expenses

JOHN   I'm very grateful.

LEILA   You're seeing the world.

JOHN   The world. Yeah.

         But what I mean is

LEILA   Have you seen my scarf?

JOHN   do we have to say goodbye at the airport?

LEILA   Black silk, swore I had it on the plane

JOHN   Does it really fucking matter which fucking scarf or which fucking shoes you wear to a fucking meeting?

         A look – rage.

LEILA   Everything matters.

         Everything I wear or don't wear is seen as a statement. Everything I say or do or fail to say or do is ammunition.

         If I'm late to a meeting, if I get drunk after a conference, if I wear an ill-fitting suit, if I bring a man to a client dinner

JOHN   The way you talk it's like you're going into battle.

LEILA   Shoes matter. Covering my neck

         matters.

         I don't expect you to understand.

         She picks up the guest phone. Dials and waits.

         (*Into phone.*) Yes I'd like a car for as soon as possible.

JOHN   Chaotic. Unpredictable. Counterintuitive.

LEILA   Excuse me?

JOHN   Just googling nonlinear dynamics.

         *

LEILA   Can you sing?

JOHN   Very badly.

LEILA   And the French?

JOHN   (*In French*.) Terrible.

        What?

LEILA   Nothing, just

        Crossing time zones. It's like time stands still, it's like
        we're chasing time or time's chasing us, it's

        Unsustainable.

*

He's holding a camera.

JOHN   I went shopping.

LEILA   So I see.

JOHN   It's a Canon EOS and it's got an ISO range of up to
        fifty thousand.

LEILA   That money was to

JOHN   cover my rent this month, I know, but, I wanna take
        photos. Real photos. I was thinking of doing an online
        course. Seems like a waste of an experience, visiting
        all these places and not recording any of it.

LEILA   Well, sounds like a fun hobby.

JOHN   I'm serious, I think this could be my Thing

        He points the camera at her.

LEILA   No, don't, I don't like having my picture taken.

JOHN   But I bought a camera!

LEILA   Photograph the view.

JOHN   You are the view!

LEILA   I'm serious, John, get that thing away from me.

He persists. Gets up close.

JOHN   I've been reading about composition and light – God
        you're really fucking sexy, no you are, and not just
        for your

        She slaps him across the face – hard.

*

She's holding a paper bag.

LEILA   I went shopping.

JOHN   So I see.

LEILA   Here.

JOHN   Oh, you

        didn't have to but

LEILA   I wanted to.

JOHN   Thanks.

        Thank you.

LEILA   Well?

        Aren't you going to try them on?

        He pulls the clothes out the bag.

JOHN   Nice.

        Fuck me. Seventy euro for a pair of boxers?

        Oh, you want me to

        Right now?

LEILA   Would you like a drink first?

        No. He starts undressing.

        She watches him. He can feel her watching him.

        *Pauses while he's stark bollock naked. Wonders, is this
        a good moment to*

No. That would be fucking weird.

He tries on his new clothes.

JOHN   Yeah?

LEILA   Yeah.

JOHN   They fit.

LEILA   I chose well.

JOHN   You did.

So does this mean I can go to the dinner with you?

LEILA   What?

JOHN   You said there was a dinner.

LEILA   There is but

it's shop talk, you'd be bored to death.

JOHN   Or maybe I wouldn't. Maybe I'd learn something.

LEILA   Would do you good to get out.

JOHN

LEILA   Eiffel Tower, Moulin Rouge, eat some cheese, I don't
know

JOHN   They'll laugh at me.

LEILA   Who's they?

JOHN   The French.

LEILA

JOHN   When I try and actually speak, my throat tightens up,
my palms

LEILA   For God's sake.

JOHN   Yeah, no, you're right.

He picks up the camera.

LEILA   Be careful.

JOHN   Bit of sun never

LEILA   There's a red-level warning.

JOHN   Paris is burning, is it?

LEILA   I'll call you a car.

JOHN   Think I'll just jump on a

LEILA   No, of course, it's

up to you, if you want to die of heatstroke

JOHN   I like heat.

He turns to leave.

Stops. Snaps a photo of her face.

She freezes – helpless.

*

JOHN   What did he do to you?

LEILA   It happened. I was there. He Did To Me – I don't

That's not how I choose to think about it.

JOHN   If I'd known, when I had the ice bucket, when I was
this close

LEILA

JOHN   Said you liked it. The violence.

LEILA   I did. I do. But.

*

JOHN   I'm sweating.

LEILA   Said you liked it. The heat.

JOHN   I do. I did. But.

Her phone buzzes. She looks but doesn't answer.

Who's that?

LEILA   No one.

JOHN   Who's no one?

LEILA   What?

JOHN   What?

LEILA   You should have a shower.

*

JOHN   I just had a massage and it was one hundred per cent
The best thing that's ever happened to my body.

Apart from you.

Lonely Planet says there are five hundred and twelve
things to do in Mumbai and I only managed one.
Massage wasn't even on the list.

I took a few photos. I'm learning about mastering
light. Feels good to be honing a skill. I'd like to learn
a language too, like actually learn a language. Keep
meaning to learn Spanish, no wait, French, but then

I dunno. Life takes over.

That shower is fantastic by the way.

LEILA   You're in a good mood.

JOHN   I am, I'm in an excellent mood because I gave that
money you gave me to a blind woman in the street.

LEILA   What?

JOHN   I said

LEILA   That was quite a lot of money.

JOHN   For her, yeah, loads, I think it could really turn her life
around.

LEILA   That money was

JOHN   to cover my food and travel, I know, but I walked,
walking's free, and I ate street food, pani puri, which is
Real as well as cheap.

LEILA   Still poisoning tourists, even in a drought.

JOHN   I have a strong stomach, I used to eat leftover canapés
        when I worked at the hotel, like even old prawns

LEILA   And so what you just give the rest of the cash to the
        first beggar you see?

JOHN   She was blind!

LEILA   You're the one who's blind. She was probably forced
        into it, deliberately maimed as a child, she's probably
        given it all to her ringleader, you have No idea where
        that money is going, what sort of criminal activity it's
        funding – cartels, human trafficking

JOHN   You're in a bad mood.

LEILA   I am, I'm in an awful mood because one of the largest
        professional services networks in the world can't raise
        even a quarter of what it needs to fund sustainable
        initiatives in developing countries

JOHN   Okay but

LEILA   and it's those very countries that are on the front line
        of climate impacts, which has a knock-on effect for
        businesses

JOHN   That has nothing to do with

LEILA   It has everything to do with

JOHN   Who chopped down their forests and stole their oil and
        imported Coca-Cola?

LEILA   Oh and You're saving the planet by giving My money
        to beggars?

JOHN   I never said I was saving the planet, that is not
        something I said.

        I was trying to do a good thing.

LEILA   Well. I hope you feel good about yourself.

JOHN   I do. I feel excellent about myself. Thanks.

*

JOHN   I thought maybe we could fuck.

LEILA

JOHN   Fucking sometimes helps, in these situations.

        I mean it's not going to decarbonise the global
        economy or whatever you call it but

LEILA   I'm not feeling especially horny right now.

        Maybe if you

JOHN   Sorry.

LEILA   Don't

JOHN   No, I'm an idiot and that was an idiotic thing to do and
        it won't happen again, it's your money

LEILA   It's not about the money.

JOHN   and I'm fine with women paying for stuff

LEILA   Stop talking.

JOHN   Okay.

LEILA   You're still talking.

JOHN   What are you

LEILA   (*Whispered.*) Shut up.

        A look – electric.

        Wait.

JOHN   Can't promise a feeling.

*

Lightning strikes.

LEILA   It'll fade once we're back. The shivers. That feeling in
        your chest.

JOHN   Is that how it works?

LEILA   Until next time. That's how it has to work. That's
the deal.

JOHN   Deal.

LEILA   You carry on with your life and I

*

JOHN   You have Great hair.

LEILA   Thank you.

*

JOHN   (*Reading from his phone*.) With its extremes of poverty
and wealth, its brash get-ahead culture and the
presence of illegal firearms, it's hardly surprising that
the city can be a dangerous place.

How am I supposed to take photos if I can't walk
down the street?

LEILA   It might have escaped your notice but we

I am here for a policy dialogue stakeholder
consultation, not a holiday

JOHN   No, no that hadn't escaped my notice

LEILA   and there is a lot at stake

JOHN   it's just that Cape Town

LEILA   and I can't exactly ask the South African government
to move their annual general meeting to Cape Town
just to suit my

JOHN

LEILA   Our latest report shows that

JOHN   Your what.

LEILA   things are changing.

JOHN   Go on, what do you call me?

LEILA   I call you John.

JOHN   when people ask, people must've asked, colleagues, clients

LEILA   People should mind their own business.

JOHN   What am I supposed to call You? What do I tell my friends? my dad? That you're mine, here, in this room, within these walls, but once we're through border control we're strangers again?

LEILA   We talked about this, John.

JOHN   I know. You pay. My flights, my expenses, I'm very grateful.

LEILA   I can't

mother you, that's not part of the

JOHN   Deal.

LEILA   Look I'm sorry but your ego is just going to have to look after itself today.

*

JOHN   It's the in-between times.

I thought I'd use those to apply for jobs, I mean real jobs, jobs that are in some way meaningful or fulfilling, like yours, you know, saving the planet with your adaptation and litigation

LEILA   Mitigation and in any case it's too late for

JOHN   (*Talking over her.*) and legislation and gas monitoring and stakeholder bollocks but it's hard. It's hard because a) my CV is shit and b) most jobs aren't flexible enough that I can fuck off every couple of weeks to follow you around the world

LEILA   I wouldn't call a few business trips following me around the world

JOHN   So I stopped looking.

Now all I do is wait.

I wait for the taxi, I wait to board the plane, I wait for
you to return from your Conferences and your Very
Important Meetings and I don't

get it, I mean you are clearly very intelligent, I mean to
the point that you make me feel stupid, so why? when
it is obvious that the companies supporting the so-
called Green Agenda are the very same companies
fucking up the earth and yeah you're a vegetarian but
we've circled the globe how many times now

LEILA   Yes because it's really that simple.

JOHN   I hate it.

LEILA   Flying?

JOHN   Capitalism.

LEILA   Right.

And I suppose you hate the pool and the spa and the
minibar – let's have a drink, oh look you finished the
Scotch.

*

JOHN   It's the in-between times. It's like time stands still, it's
like I'm chasing time or time's chasing me, it's

snapshots.

I take photos because I need evidence.

*

LEILA   You were saying?

JOHN   Do you know where I live?

LEILA

JOHN

LEILA   Ealing?

JOHN   Course you do, you always put me in the taxi first –
Acton actually, the shit bit, it's a house share, kitchen's

this big, locks on all the bedroom doors, it's six
hundred pounds a month

LEILA I know.

JOHN   Course you do, you gave me six hundred pounds to pay
the rent and I spent it on a camera. Bedroom's about a
quarter of the size of this room, door doesn't open
properly 'cause there's a wardrobe in the way, damp
patch in the corner of the ceiling but I know, I'm lucky
to have a roof over my head, I mean it's not as Lonely
Planet would put it Extreme Poverty and there are no
Illegal Firearms, at least none that I've seen, it's just
This, always being face to face with This, not exactly
homely but everything works, the light bulbs work and
the taps don't leak and whatever's going on outside if
you run out of spring water you just call down and they
bring it on a fucking tray with ice and a perfectly
symmetrical slice of lemon and I'm sure there are lots of
very nice people in the world but my housemates, the
ones I've met, they are so fucking cold and I can feel
myself freezing over, we just sit in our little boxes
ignoring each other, sometimes I imagine pulling the
roof off the building and looking down on it, all these
sad little people, separated by partitions

What was I

LEILA I don't

JOHN   but yes but you won't even tell me where you live!
I mean I know you live in London

LEILA Richmond.

JOHN   Richmond, nice, yeah, just down the road – isn't that
odd? No? I find that odd and I think other people
would too, I think

LEILA Other people should

JOHN   mind their own business, maybe, but it feels

wrong and I find myself lying, telling a series of small
lies so I don't sound crazy, like I told my dad I'm

working abroad, said I'd got this job with an international catering company, think that's what I said, showed him a few photos, he was impressed, he's never been on a plane and my friends, the ones who still bother talking to me, if I told them how it really is with you I'd sound like the biggest twat in Acton

LEILA   John.

JOHN   but now it's got to the point where I can't remember what I've said or haven't said and and and

I think about you. All the time. It's annoying the amount of time I spend thinking about you, dreaming up scenarios, imagining all the stuff we haven't done. You won't leave my head and so I fill in the gaps, I get to know you, do you know what the word Know actually means? And Adam Knew His Wife – do you have a husband? a child?

LEILA

JOHN   I have a right to know.

LEILA   Do you?

JOHN   I have

I think

I think when you invest this much

Self, you have rights, you have

you should have, should be entitled to

LEILA   Entitled.

JOHN   Yes.

LEILA   D'you see how that's a little bit

JOHN

LEILA   problematic?

JOHN   I'm going out.

LEILA   Be careful.

JOHN   I'd like to get shot.

LEILA   For God's sake.

JOHN   I love you. And now I'd like to die.

*

LEILA   Right, well

JOHN   I better

LEILA   Probably for the best.

JOHN   Probably is.

*

LEILA   You promised.

        You promised you wouldn't

JOHN   Can't promise a feeling.

*

LEILA   I just got a call from London.

JOHN   How is London?

LEILA   Things are changing.

JOHN   You mean

        heat? drought? Genocide?

LEILA   The firm.

JOHN   Right.

LEILA   That man you hit over the head with the ice bucket

JOHN   the cunt?

LEILA   He resigned.

JOHN   Why?

LEILA   People started talking about it.

JOHN   Good.

LEILA   Women.

JOHN

LEILA   I didn't but

        I should have but

        I didn't.

        So anyway, I'm up for partner.

JOHN   Congrats.

LEILA   Thank you.

JOHN   Partner. Wow. Sounds important.

LEILA   It is important. People don't want to believe what's happening. The flooding, the wildfires, if people can't see it

JOHN   D'you get a pay rise?

LEILA   Panel's next month but yes, I expect they'll double my salary, give me some shares

JOHN   That's cool.

        I mean you already earn

        a lot, so double that, that's

        a lot a lot.

LEILA   I work hard.

        I work hard and work isn't just about the hours you put in, it isn't just clocking on and clocking off

JOHN   No, I know

LEILA   and it's especially hard when the President of the United States is a climate-change-denying predator.

JOHN   We should celebrate. Do something. What d'you
         wanna do?

LEILA   I want to get drunk.

JOHN   Okay.

LEILA   I want to order the most disgustingly overpriced bottle
         of champagne they've got and I want to get horribly
         horribly drunk.

*

Champagne cork pops.

JOHN   You were right, the other room was shit, you couldn't
         see shit.

         This. This is a view.

LEILA   Pass me that.

         She drinks straight from the bottle.

JOHN   Careful, you're spilling

LEILA   I'll order another.

JOHN   I don't like waste.

LEILA   You're already wasted.

JOHN   Can't stand

         No I mean waste as in

LEILA   I'm hot, are you hot?

JOHN   It's hot, yeah.

LEILA   Is the air-con working?

JOHN   No. Please. Don't let's change again.

LEILA   If the air-con isn't working

JOHN   then we'll just be hot.

LEILA   I'm thirsty, are you thirsty?

JOHN   Water, here

       She doesn't take it.

LEILA   It really is stiflingly hot in here.

JOHN   Take something off.

LEILA   You take it off.

       A look – electric.

       Wait.

*

JOHN   I waited for you, then I looked for you, then I waited
       for terrible news because in case you hadn't noticed
       there are lots of terrible things happening in the world

*

LEILA   My purse, there, in my bag

JOHN   What?

LEILA   Open it.

JOHN   Why?

LEILA   You'll see.

       He looks in her handbag.

JOHN   Did you

       order drugs?

LEILA   Excuse me?

JOHN   No I mean I'm totally up for

LEILA   Drugs? in my purse?

JOHN   If that's the vibe

LEILA   are you out of your mind?

*

JOHN   I don't know, it's a foreign country, anything could've
        happened and speaking of my app, Lonely Planet says
        that lockdown or no lockdown it's not advisable for
        women to travel unaccompanied late at night.

*

LEILA   Well?

JOHN   There's

        nothing here, just

        lots and lots of

        cash – why are you carrying so much cash, this is like

LEILA   a million yen.

JOHN   Right, which is

LEILA   Take it.

JOHN

LEILA   Buy something.

JOHN   But

        everything's on the room.

LEILA   I'm not.

JOHN

LEILA   I'm in the room, I'm not on the room.

JOHN   I don't

LEILA   Yes you do, you understand perfectly.

JOHN   Wait, so you want me to

LEILA

JOHN   pay you?

LEILA

JOHN   Okay.

LEILA   I want to be bought.

JOHN   Bought.

Huh.

Like a

LEILA   Yes.

JOHN   Okay.

LEILA   Is it? okay?

JOHN

LEILA

JOHN   Sorry.

LEILA   Don't

apologise.

He looks in the mirror. Touches his face.

What are you doing?

JOHN   Do I look blurry to you?

*

BUTLER *enters with a trolley.*

He sets down a plate. Lifts its dome cover. Reveals a rare steak, perfectly cooked.

She tips him.

He nods thank you. Exits.

LEILA   I've had these cravings.

Meat. Something that lived. Something that had a heart.

She picks up the steak. Holds it in her hands. Looks at it closely, examining the squidgy flesh, the marbled fat, the blood in the cracks.

Puts it back down. Wipes her hands clean on a napkin.
Cuts herself a small piece with a knife and fork. Holds
it to her mouth. Takes a bite.

Heaven.

Another bite.

JOHN *watches her. She can feel him watching her.*

He goes to her. Kneels down. Starts gently biting at
her thighs.

*

In the same position.

JOHN My dad's in hospital.

   He had a a a

   stroke, or something, he

   I can't remember the name of it but it's like a

   blood clot, or something? like a fat globule, a globule
   of fat gets trapped inside a blood vessel and

   Yeah.

   I didn't visit because it would've meant missing
   our flight.

LEILA

JOHN It's okay. He said he's very happy for me. Very pleased
   I'm getting to see the world. And stuff.

LEILA Streets are on lockdown so you won't be seeing much
   of the world this week.

JOHN It's fine. I'll go when we get back.

   She pecks him on the head. Gently moves him out the
   way. Stands up.

LEILA Might as well practise your Spanish while you're here.

JOHN French, I'm learning

   French.

*

JOHN   Where have you been?

          I've been looking for you.

          All night I've been looking for you, in the bar and the
          pool and the gym and your phone? what's that about?
          Just disappearing all night with no phone and no Don't
          tell me you were with those suits because I looked and
          they were all there, still are, in the bar downstairs so
          don't give me any of that because That wasn't part of
          the deal.

LEILA   Deal.

JOHN   We talked about this, Leila.

LEILA   I went out. You could go out too, you're not a prisoner
          in this room.

JOHN   Streets are on lockdown you said.

LEILA   That was last month, Johannesburg, Jesus Christ, just
          sitting here all day and all night, what about your app?

JOHN   I wasn't just Sitting Here, I was looking for you.
          I waited for you, then I looked for you, then I waited
          for terrible news because in case you hadn't noticed
          there are lots of terrible things happening in the world
          right now and I was worried, I thought you might've

LEILA

JOHN   I dunno, got caught in a storm, stuck in a cave, dragged
          out to sea – I don't know, it's a foreign country,
          anything could've happened and speaking of my app,
          Lonely Planet says that lockdown or no lockdown it is
          not advisable for women to travel unaccompanied late
          at night.

LEILA   Right. Well. You can tell Lonely Planet, from me, to
          fuck off.

JOHN

LEILA   Would do you good to get out.

JOHN   They'll eat me alive.

LEILA   Who's they?

JOHN   The mosquitoes!

LEILA

JOHN   It's hotter, it's wetter

LEILA   Yes I'd noticed.

JOHN   Half the world has dengue fever

LEILA   You're exaggerating, you should stop reading those articles.

JOHN   Insect-borne diseases are a Thing and people are Dying.

LEILA   Bangkok for God's sake! Go outside, see it, smell it, feel it

JOHN   I can see it and smell it from here and it stinks – what happened to your knee?

She opens the minibar.

LEILA   Did you finish the Scotch?

JOHN   Leila?

LEILA   I fucked someone.

Someone fucked me.

I know, that wasn't the

JOHN   What happens in London

LEILA   Not London. Here. Now. In Patpong.

JOHN   But

I was waiting for you.

LEILA   I know.

JOHN   Patpong?

LEILA   Yeah.

JOHN   Sounds like a made-up place.

She opens a mini-bottle of red wine. Drinks straight from the bottle. Spills some down her chin. Wipes it off with the back of her hand.

This is one of your little fantasies, isn't it. 'I want to be bought'

LEILA   For a while I just stood there, watching.

The men walk in packs. They all look the same, they've become the same animal, burnt faces, beer bellies, fading tattoos. And there's this

fascinating sense of entitlement

JOHN   Entitlement.

LEILA   as they walk down that strip, this ability to completely suspend their disbelief, they feel like

gods, they've saved all year for a trip to Thailand with the lads and fuck the rain, they're used to rain, and buying a girl in Patpong, well it's not all that different to buying a kebab on the way home.

Hungry. Bit peckish.

JOHN   Why are you telling me this?

LEILA   I caught one when he strayed from his pack. Pretended I couldn't speak English. Gave him a good price, more like a portion of chips than a kebab and he shrugged, which meant yes

JOHN   I don't believe you, you're exaggerating, you're scaremongering me.

LEILA   Could've bought any one of those girls but he bought me. Round the back of a karaoke bar and a woman inside was singing 'Hey Jude' like she was being strangled and I thought maybe this is what the end of

the world sounds like and I stood against the wall, skirt
around my waist, his sour beer breath right up in
my face

JOHN   Shut up.

LEILA   I'm telling you this because you asked.

JOHN   Shut up.

LEILA   You asked what happened to my knee, I haven't got to
the bit where he

JOHN   Shut up shut up shut up shut up shut up shut up shut up

LEILA   (*Talking over him.*) After he'd finished he gave me a pat
on the head.

Like he'd done a good thing, like he was helping me
out, helping out the economy.

She catches sight of herself in the mirror.

Jesus Christ, look at the state of me, I look like a
streetwalker, it's this wet heat, it does this to my hair.

JOHN   Streetwalkers can't afford dresses like that.

LEILA   No, I don't suppose they can.

Still. I'll wash it. My hair. And the rest of me.

JOHN   My head hurts.

LEILA   Just sitting here all day and all night, drinking yourself
to death – what about your photos? what about
learning Spanish?

He sees red.

Grabs the camera.

Whacks it repeatedly on the floor.

JOHN   FRENCH.

FRENCH.

I'M LEARNING

FUCKING

FRENCH.

And so on until the scene smashes into pieces.

*

She turns off the TV with a remote. Noise continues from outside – quiet at first.

JOHN   I was watching that.

He flops down on the bed.

She paces – restless.

Opens a bag of nuts.

LEILA   Want one?

He shakes his head.

JOHN   Actually yeah, go on.

Opens his mouth.

She drops a nut into it.

A memory – bitter.

He spits it out.

Karaoke.

LEILA   There aren't any karaoke bars in Cancún.

JOHN   What, none? Not a single karaoke bar in the whole of Cancún?

LEILA   I mean it's not a Thing, not like

JOHN   Don't Mexican people like to sing?

LEILA   in Asia, it's

Never mind.

JOHN   When shit gets bad, people sing. When the world ends, people will die singing – you'll know things are bad when I start to sing.

*

JOHN   If the world ends I want it to be here, with you.

LEILA   The world won't end. Not yet.

JOHN   I don't want this to end. This moment I mean, not

LEILA   It feels like this because it isn't real.

*

He goes to pick up the

JOHN   Huh.

LEILA   What?

JOHN   No, just

         Nothing.

         Finds the real phone. Dials and waits.

         (*Into phone.*) Yeah d'you do eggs Benedict?

         Oh.

         Okay.

         No, it's fine.

         Thanks.

         Hangs up.

LEILA

JOHN   They've run out of eggs.

*

She opens the minibar.

LEILA   They've run out of Scotch.

         There's a warm beer. You might as well drink it.

JOHN   Yeah I used to have a thing about finishing drinks. Couldn't leave a pub without downing a pint or necking the dregs of someone else's glass of wine.

But these days I'm really laidback about it.

These days I might be drinking a beer and then halfway through drinking it I might change my mind and decide I want

a Scotch, for example, and I'll just

leave the beer and order a Scotch.

LEILA   They've run out of Scotch.

JOHN   For example.

Same goes for food. My dad was always 'waste not want not' and 'finish what's on your plate or you won't get pudding'. He always made me feel like

we were lucky. That there were people in the world who didn't have what we had and so the act of not finishing, it was

I dunno. Disrespectful.

And I always finished what was on my plate 'cause I always wanted pudding, and because you don't question those things when you're a kid. But that whole way of thinking, it's completely illogical, I mean

Waste is waste, whether it's moving through your gut or rotting in a bin.

*

JOHN   What was I

LEILA   We are living in a much more challenging future.

Heat. Drought. Flooding. Environmental refugees

JOHN   Oh yeah. Extinction.

LEILA   and then I talk a bit about climate genocide and businesses engaging in materially relevant areas and the removal of industrial emissions and

JOHN   Isn't it a bit late for all that?

LEILA   I'm building to the Green Agenda

JOHN   I know but you've been building to the Green Agenda
your whole career and things are getting

LEILA   This is about thinking long term and acting short term.

JOHN   You've said that before

LEILA   It's punchy. It's a good line to end on.

JOHN   and I didn't used to understand it but

Apply it to you and me

LEILA   I'm not talking about you and me, I'm talking about
the bigger picture.

JOHN   You know when you practise your speeches on me
I'm not really listening.

LEILA   No?

JOHN   No. I just like looking at you. I like the way your
mouth moves.

LEILA   I'm tired, this is

tiring

*

JOHN   This is fine, this is more than fine

LEILA   (*Into phone.*) Yes I'd like to speak to the manager.

JOHN   No. Please. Don't let's change again.

LEILA   I work hard.

JOHN   I know you do, I'm not

LEILA   I work hard and the work I do is important, it has an
impact on the bigger picture and what I mean by
Bigger Picture is that yes you might give a wad of cash
to a blind beggar in the street and feel good about

yourself for a day and yes you might post a selfie of you and a boy with no shoes on but those small isolated gestures don't mean anything, in fact I'd say they are more damaging than doing nothing because at least nothing isn't claiming to be something, at least nothing isn't skewing the bigger picture.

So forgive me if I'm a little picky about the hotel I stay at and the wine I drink and the food I eat and forgive my enormous salary and my higher-than-average carbon footprint but while you lie on your back with the curtains drawn I'm out there making billion-dollar decisions that affect our children and our children's children and

JOHN   Children.

LEILA   I'm not talking about myself, I'm talking about

JOHN   Alright. Forgiven. Absolved.

LEILA   (*Into phone.*) I'm sorry?

Oh.

Okay.

No, it's not fine.

She hangs up.

JOHN

LEILA   I think I'm allowed

I am allowing myself

to have done what I did.

*

JOHN   He's dead. He died.

LEILA

JOHN   My dad.

LEILA   I'm

JOHN

LEILA   sorry, I

   really am sorry to hear that.

JOHN   Sorry.

   Huh.

LEILA   I don't know what else

JOHN   Yeah. Well.

LEILA   Is there a

   memorial or

JOHN   Yeah.

LEILA

JOHN   Well.

LEILA   Well?

JOHN   Depends.

   Depends when we're

   when I'm back.

LEILA   You know you can

JOHN   Yup.

LEILA   leave any time, I can

JOHN   I know.

LEILA   pay

JOHN   Thanks.

   Thank you.

   Thought I'd make a

LEILA

JOHN   speech, thought maybe

LEILA

JOHN   you could help me?

LEILA   Right.

Yes. Yes of course.

What do you want to say?

*

JOHN   Is that a

LEILA

JOHN   crack, is that

The mirror, I think it's

LEILA   John.

JOHN   Hm?

LEILA   The speech.

JOHN   What?

LEILA   You wanted to

JOHN   speak.

LEILA   Yes.

JOHN   Right.

But I

Yes.

But I

Hm.

*

JOHN   Hm?

LEILA   I said you're sweating.

JOHN   They're attracted to sweat.

LEILA   John.

JOHN   Sweat. Heat. The hotter the skin, the older the sweat

LEILA   There aren't any mosquitoes in Moscow.

JOHN   What, none? Not a single mosquito in the whole of
Don't Indian bugs like to bite?

LEILA   I said Moscow, not

*

JOHN   Stop

tricking me, we are in

Istanbul and we have changed rooms Three times
already and now we're back in the first one because
you are

LEILA   How would you describe me?

JOHN   You're crazy, you're a crazed woman, there is
something

wrong, something went wrong, somewhere, I'm

thirsty, are you thirsty?

LEILA   Water, here.

He takes it.

JOHN   (*Quietly.*) Whore.

LEILA   What?

JOHN   Nothing.

Sorry.

Forgiven. Absolved.

I'm sorry.

Thanks.

Thank you.

He drinks the water.

*

LEILA   Say it.

JOHN

LEILA   I want to hear you say it.

JOHN   I'm not a child.

LEILA   And I'm not

        mothering you, that's not

JOHN   Addis Ababa.

LEILA   No John, we're in Brussels

JOHN   Again?

LEILA   and I have a meeting to go to

JOHN   Another one?

LEILA   and this meeting could actually change the shape of the world, like geometrically alter the shape of the planet, so you see it's really quite

JOHN   important.

LEILA   Quite.

*

JOHN   Partner. Wow. Sounds important.

LEILA   It is important. People don't want to believe what's happening. The wars, the mass migration, if people can't see it

*

LEILA   Say it.

JOHN   Doha.

LEILA   No John

JOHN   Dubai.

LEILA   we're in Washington

JOHN   Washington? Cool!

LEILA   and I have a meeting to go to

JOHN   and this meeting could actually

LEILA   change things, yes

JOHN   Right, like ice caps and sea levels and the ozone layer and

LEILA   the future of the human race, yes

JOHN   Future of the human race? Cool!

LEILA   so you see it's really quite

JOHN   important?

LEILA   Quite.

*

Noise from outside grows louder.

JOHN   How will you get to the meeting?

LEILA   It's not a meeting, it's a conference.

JOHN   How will you get to the

LEILA   In an armoured vehicle.

JOHN   There's a red-level warning.

LEILA   Well I can't save the planet from a hotel room.

JOHN   D'you still think you can do that?

LEILA   I think that the worse it gets, the more they look to me, the higher I climb, the more I earn and I know that sounds awful but

JOHN   You're the fucking expert.

LEILA   but I still think there's hope.

JOHN

LEILA

JOHN   Stories keep coming up on my feed. Pacific Islands uninhabitable, parts of Bangladesh under water

Even Texas, Florida, California – imagine! American refugees!

LEILA   You should stop reading those articles.

JOHN   Hard to know what's real and what's fake.

LEILA   You should stop worrying so much.

JOHN   But there is so Much to worry about, like

Insect-borne diseases, they're a Thing now, half the world has what's-it-called, especially in Madrid

LEILA   Milan, we're in

JOHN   It's hotter, it's wetter, it's Louder

He goes to open the

Huh.

LEILA

JOHN   No, just

I thought there was a door here.

LEILA

JOHN   Huh.

Her phone buzzes. She looks but doesn't answer.

Who's that?

LEILA   No one.

JOHN   Who's no one?

LEILA   What?

JOHN   What?

LEILA   You should get some sleep.

He tries to grab the phone. She catches his arm.

*

Lightning strikes.

JOHN   When you touch me I get these shivers.

LEILA   When you shiver I

something

in my chest – fuck, that sounds

JOHN   I'm sure it's normal, just

I can't remember it

happening

before

LEILA   These Midwestern storms, they're

JOHN   intense.

LEILA   If the world ends

JOHN   If the world ends we'll move to that house on the
farm and

LEILA   disappear

JOHN   together.

I have these dreams, sometimes I can't tell if I'm

LEILA   You're asleep.

We're asleep, I think.

And that house on the farm

isn't real.

He slaps himself across the face.

*

LEILA   You've been forgetting things.

Big things like time and place

JOHN   We're in a hotel. We're always in a hotel. And each room is exactly the same as the last room, and the one before that, and the one before that, like even the position of the bed and the window and

It's difficult sometimes, to remember where and when and

how and why and who and what when there are

There are precisely one hundred and ninety-five countries in the world, unless you don't count Taiwan in which case there are one hundred and ninety-four and even without Taiwan that is a Lot for the brain to choose from and from where I'm lying they all look pretty similar.

Have we been to Taiwan?

*

JOHN   I'm feeling a lot better.

They did some tests and it's not dengue fever.

LEILA   I told you it wasn't.

JOHN   So there's nothing wrong.

LEILA   Good.

JOHN   So we can just

go back to normal.

LEILA

JOHN   Except that there is

something

wrong, something went wrong, somewhere, I'm

LEILA   Shh.

*

LEILA   Did you go?

JOHN

LEILA   The memorial. Did you make a speech?

JOHN

LEILA

JOHN   Yeah.

LEILA   And?

JOHN   And I think that might be the first time you've asked me anything about my life.

But I don't want to talk about death.

*

BUTLER *enters – out of breath, uniform dirty and ripped, holding a raw steak.*

She takes it and tips him.

He nods thank you.

JOHN   What's it like out there?

He stares. Says nothing. Exits.

LEILA   I've had these cravings.

She takes a bite.

And another and another and with each bite she becomes more animal. Blood drips down her chin. She doesn't wipe it off.

JOHN *watches her. She can no longer feel him watching her.*

She finishes – satisfied.

They tripled my salary, gave me some shares

JOHN   That's

cool.

LEILA   The amount of money I earn, I mean it's disgusting.

I'm starting to wonder if I'm not just a very well-paid tick-box on a very lucrative checklist.

It really is disgusting, the amount of money I earn.

He shrugs.

Thought you hated it.

JOHN   Money?

LEILA   Capitalism.

JOHN   It isn't black and white.

LEILA   No?

JOHN   Where there's money there's influence there's change.

That's what you told me.

You've got a

Blood on her chin.

LEILA   Oh.

JOHN   Here, let me

He wipes it off.

*

Karaoke track to 'Hey Jude' plays, drowning out the noise from outside.

He sings a few lines, like he's being strangled.

She turns off the TV with a remote.

LEILA   Things are bad but they're not that bad.

*

JOHN   I followed you.

Can't remember where we'd

Moscow, Mumbai, Madrid, Milan, we said goodbye at Heathrow and I got that feeling in my chest I always get when we say goodbye, not allowed to kiss you once we're through customs, and I told my driver to follow your driver and when we pulled up at the house

I waited. I watched you wheel your case to the door.
Watched you turn the key in the lock. Saw a window
light up – kitchen, maybe? and you looked so small
and so alone and I wanted to come inside and put my
arms around you and

There was someone else.

If I'd had a gun I would have shot myself.

LEILA   You promised

You promised you wouldn't

JOHN   There was someone else.

A young man. Blurry.

For a second I thought it was Me. I thought I was
seeing my reflection.

*

*Powercut. Dim flickering of lights. Noise from outside grows
louder.*

YOUNG MAN *sits between her legs. Or maybe he's just the
shadow of a man, not physically there. She strokes his head –
big cat protecting her cub.*

JOHN *watches from the door.*

*

Lights return to normal. YOUNG MAN/*his shadow has
disappeared.*

JOHN   Who is he?

a lover? a son?

LEILA   You're imagining it. Like you imagine we're
somewhere else, like you imagine the room has
changed shape and the door has disappeared and the
world is about to end.

JOHN   I have a right to know.

LEILA   Do you?

JOHN   I have

I think when you invest this much

Self, you have rights, you have

LEILA   This isn't a transaction.

JOHN   but you like things to be clear.

LEILA

JOHN   So. Your story. Your choice. You get to choose.

Us or the world. You can't save both so which do you choose.

Okay.

LEILA   Really I've

got enough to worry about with this speech and

JOHN   Okay.

He turns to leave.

Stops.

Sorry

can I just

Who are you?

*

JOHN   Well it was nice to meet you

LEILA   Leila.

JOHN   John.

*

LEILA   John.

JOHN   No.

LEILA   Please.

JOHN   You've taken

everything.

LEILA   I paid for

JOHN   No.

LEILA   everything.

JOHN   I paid, I'm the one who

LEILA   Your camera, your clothes, that procedure to fix your swollen turbinate

JOHN   You took and you took and you might as well have eaten me alive – what do you want? my flesh? my blood? Here. Have it. It's yours.

He holds out his arms. Surrenders himself.

For a moment it looks like she'll devour him.

*

A snapshot – evidence.

*

JOHN   I have one photo of you. I took it without your consent. Paris I think – was it Paris? That time you slapped me. I should delete it. Doesn't feel right, owning that split second. But it's the only thing I have of you.

I look at it whenever we're apart, in the in-between times, a memory, saved. Your expression, it's weak, helpless, like I'm about to

You don't look like you.

You look like a victim.

Like prey.

*

LEILA   I'm not an egg.

a china doll.

If you smash me I won't break.

*

JOHN   I was trying to work out how long

Because it feels like I've lost years. Decades.

This

what I'm doing

what I'm about to do

is about thinking long term and acting short term.

He turns to leave.

Stops.

People are always saying carpe diem, seize the day,
live each moment to the full, grab life by the bollocks,
I didn't finish the online photography course and never
learnt any French and I'm completely in love with you,
in fact I think loving you is the only thing I've ever
managed to see through, to the point that I can't any
more. I'm spent.

How do you do it?

LEILA

JOHN   It's like you've got an extra layer of muscle or skin or

How do you live like that?

LEILA   It's the only way I can survive in this world.

I don't expect you to understand.

Be careful.

A look – longing.

JOHN   It's a waste, isn't it. This.

He exits.

She panics. Stops breathing.

Suddenly inhales.

Picks up her phone and dials.

LEILA   (*Into phone.*) It's me.

Are you there?

I'm sorry I haven't

The air-con stopped working but

It's fine.

There's a conference, they're sending an armoured vehicle so it's

I'm okay. I mean

I'm alive.

(*Laughing.*) Obviously.

I'd like to speak to him.

Call me? please?

Hangs up.

Noise from outside grows louder

and louder

and louder

She paces – restless.

(*Barely audible.*) Put simply, the Green Agenda gives you, the company

Put simply, the Green Agenda gives you the chance to invest in sustainable activities while at the same time

Bigger Picture.

I'm talking about

She stops. Listens.

Hello?

Suddenly seems very small and very alone. And like a china doll, might break.

Hello?

She opens a mini-bottle of champagne. Drinks straight from the bottle.

Noise from outside grows even louder.

Blackout.

End.

www.nickhernbooks.co.uk

facebook.com/nickhernbooks

twitter.com/nickhernbooks